DANGER FACE

DANGER FACE

C.W. Emerson

WAYFARER BOOKS
ABIQUIU, NEW MEXICO

WWW.WAYFARERBOOKS.ORG

Published in 2025 by Wayfarer Books
Cover Design and Interior Design by Connor Wolfe
TRADE PAPERBACK 9781965320891

10 9 8 7 6 5 4 3 2 1

Look for our titles in paperback, ebook, and audiobook wherever books are sold.
Wholesale offerings for retailers available through Ingram.

Wayfarer Books is committed to ecological stewardship.
We greatly value the natural environment and invest in conservation.

PO Box 1109, Abiquiu, New Mexico
wayfarer@homeboundpublications.com
WAYFARERBOOKS.ORG & WAYFARERMAGAZINE.COM

—for Scott Robert Gordon

CONTENTS

I

II

III

IV

Once or twice in his life, a man
is peeled like apples.

  —ILYA KAMINSKY, "MUSICA HUMANA"

DES RÊVES FANTASTIQUES *(Les Fantômes)*

Perhaps I dream of the dead
because there's a severance to be paid,
after a time of patient waiting;

>> a reprieve, an anointing,
>> aspirational, archangelic—

deliverance from a hostile dreamscape,
alone in the face of acrimony—

punitive actions taken against me,
yet unaware of my offense.

Perhaps the dreams are a phantom's handwork—

>> unconscious, inchoate,
>> and so, unspoken—

the aftermath of some malfeasance
by Cousin Frank or Uncle Ben,

from sword or pen of Jeremiah Locke,
the domestic deeds of Annie Laurie, Mercie Peer,
>>>> a random daughter, son.

Perhaps the act in question was mine
and mine alone; and so,

the dreams of rejection, dismissal,
betrayal by once-beloved figures

will continue unabated—
episodic, predictable,

each night, every night,

swimming a river of smoke.

THE GOSPEL ACCORDING
TO MERCIE PEER

I never once asked you to tell me you loved me. Together we had five boys and nearly sixty patents. To me, that seemed like quite enough.

Still, with your death coming only weeks after we lost Fred James, I nearly lost my mind, it's true, went running down the street screaming, as if my hair were on fire. Sybil and Jamie were there that night. It was Nurse Sybil who found you, sitting in your chair. Thanks be to God for removing me from the path of that discovery. There are still some miracles left in this faithless world.

As for our marriage, I never doubted you, never sought to dampen your enthusiasm or lay down rules. We were always companionable, even when we disagreed. I knew who you were, and how you functioned. We were partners, dear Fred, from the start.

You left me undisturbed, up reading until all hours, whilst you arose each morning at 4 a.m., your mind already humming with ideas, the laboratory your sanctuary, with Fred James only steps behind, your best erstwhile mate.

*

What can I say about the way men run the world, how things come to be what they are, how life and death dole out their random blessings and curses? How could we have raised other than five heathen boys, with the way we thought, flouted convention, denied authority? How could I lose all but one to a weakness of the heart?

Life is precious, time fleeting. Two summers ago, I myself passed from this world at Ash Grove, the lake cottage we both loved so much. Sybil attended to the practical needs of the body, and Jamie took it up to Mt. Hope Crematorium, where it was burned to smoke.

On an ordinary morning the following spring, Jamie took the rowboat out to catch his breakfast of fresh perch. Floating there, somewhere near the midpoint of Canandaigua Lake, our youngest son scattered my ashes on the crisp March breeze. In this way, I departed the world as simply and suddenly as I had entered it, quiet as dust settling over the burned-out Victor homestead, the factory, the grounds.

*

Life goes on for our granddaughters and for our lost grandson, if ever he entered this world at all—a secret you and Jamie intended to keep from me always. I still pray for his unfortunate mother, whomever and wherever she may be.

You paid dearly to dispense with them, sir—but the cost was borne by me, as well. As you know, dear husband, after death the veil thins, and more is revealed.

Your devoted wife,

Mercie Peer Locke

AMERICAN SEASONS

August 1964,
western New York State:

walking the furrowed deer tracks
            out beyond the lip of the woods
on our way to play at Sonnenberg Park—

we believed those paths were Indian trails
            worn into the dirt, dividing the trees,
all the way out past a starry base of diamond

to the monkey bars, thick poles of iron
polished to a coppery sheen
            by generations of hands.

We'd shimmy our willowed bodies
from side to side, then up and up,
          catch the swinging trapeze, or not,

landing hard in a cushion of dust
imprinted with elbow and knee.

One winter, the old Academy track
froze so slick and even, a seven-foot fence
was nothing between me and that perfect ice.

I skated 'til my ankles swelled against the leather boot—

the free glide and backward cross,
the same as Great-grandfather Piet
            over Amsterdam's canals

just days before a late-spring thaw
would bless the boat trip over—

before new lake-land revealed itself,
before the line was laced with Irish;

before Annie Laurie, his last surviving child,
would be conceived in the rancid hold
                          of a transatlantic schooner.

                    *

The year of the perfect ice, I was ten.
By then, Annie Laurie was already old.

For forty-five years,
                    she'd held the light dominion
over landscapes of brawlers, whispered liaisons,

the unborn, stillborn souls disappeared
                          from sound and sight.

Most nights, she pulled her husband Dickie
out from under barstools.
                          And every spring,
she scrubbed the winter sidewalks clean
the length of Telyea Street.

                    Annie Laurie was tired.

A sullen March morning,
the day Annie Laurie didn't wake up,
                    I turned twenty-one.

Alone now, with no reason to stay,
I traded in those northern lights
                    for sodden Novembers
and run-off straight to the Malibu pier,

for the saw-edged blades
                    of Santa Ana winds,
for nights full of rumble and crack—

but nothing quells this craving
for ochre, orange,
                    the leaves, the days—

my September song plays on and on
in deep, percussive tones that ring out
here in the west, my adopted home,

                    and there in the east, ever rising:

memories burnished
                    by autumn's umber,
gilded with falling snow.

MY EDUCATION

I was educated for a life at racetracks, country auctions,
nickel-ante poker games—how to elicit small-town gossip
over one's lascivious nature and acts. I never learned

the names of farm machines my father sold at auction,
wouldn't know a combine from a thresher,
or for that matter, a Holstein from a Guernsey.

But put me on the backstretch of an oval track, I'll show you
what separates trotters from pacers, cheap claimers
from the imagined equine elite that never raced at Finger Lakes—

and only at a small-town track outside of Canandaigua
would I ever have been hired, at seventeen, by the Daily Racing Form
as "calltaker," taking down the trackman's call of the race,

then constructing presumed positions of each horse throughout—
a highly speculative endeavor not unlike Fantasy Football, I'm told.
I ran bets for my boss, made a killing when I bet the same.

On days when the track was dark, I'd jog my father's horses,
cool them down, at the horse barn he'd built
out behind the Auction House on Chapin Road,

the sweat of the horses seeping deep
into woolen blankets of red, black, and silver plaid,
racing colors of the Emerson clan.

On Friday nights in the back of Macri's Grocery and Deli, my mother,
Jimmy Macri, his sister Rosalie, Sue Ellen Quayle and others
gathered for their weekly poker game, with Old Man Macri looking on.

He always called my mother by her maiden name—
"Miss Locke" became "Meesa Locka"—
and she was twenty again.

There on the Macri's plush upholstered couch, I needed toothpicks
to stay awake for "Dracula's Daughter," "Fall of the House of Usher"
or some other terrifying, late-night delight.

Around that time, I also learned that cars were not mere vehicles,
but also icons of free spending, markers of independence,
potential sites of marital strife.

The day Eileen drove home from Koerner Ford
in a new, candy apple red Mustang convertible, my father said,
"Christ, Eileen, do you think we're made of money?"

But I wasn't there to hear it. Wasn't here, wasn't there, wasn't anywhere
except lost in "Bracken's World," a TV show about backstage Hollywood,
the place I truly belonged—directing from behind the camera,

or, if I grew to be handsome enough, being artfully lit
by my boyfriend, the Director of Photography.
I watched the show religiously, alone in my room

on an old black-and-white, and envisioned my glamorous future life,
where in each week's teaser, at the end of every episode, my true parentage
might finally be revealed. For having concealed nothing

of my nascent gay persona, my father had disowned me.
Eileen sent "care packages" to my tiny, basement
"garden apartment" not far from campus, in frigid St. Paul.

I continued to dream of the life I'd have—
golden tan, blond hair feathering back
in the balmy Malibu breeze. And now,

as I step outside my manufactured desert home,
the dust-dry air gathers into a *haboub*,
a storm lifting up toward the San Jacintos.

I roll up the windows of my 2003 Buick Rendezvous
and hunker down, out of danger, out of sight, waiting
for the storm to come, to settle, and finally, to pass.

HOW I CAME TO BE MYSELF

—*after Justin Boening*

You remind me of myself
at twenty-five:

     electrified,

& living off stars
that fell in my hair, my eyes—

        like you,
I dreamt of infernos, fields
deliberately set aflame—

      fires kindled
by bursts of atoms
culled from summer storms.

     *

On the morning of my milestone day
I scaled the city walls, breathed
the unbreathable city air

(the fields,
   in my dreams,
     were blazing, blazing . . .)

& for crimes committed
or any conceived,

   I declared my absolution.

*

I knew that, soon, they would come for me.

I armed the doors & the paintings,
stared at my own battered face.

     I let myself dry like a dandelion.
When all but my stem had vanished,
with nothing left
          to be blown away,

     finally,   I was free.

The rest, as they say, is the rest.

ELEGY FOR DANIEL

This house I inhabit is a house of sorrow, of mourning. No one enters randomly, untallied, unaccounted for, no permission granted to leave at will. In this house, we keep our distance one from the other, for none of us believes that anyone's grief could be as deep and searing as our own.

These days, we're surrounded by songs of the dead. We mouth the words, we hum along, seeking some form of communion—for when we've been separate, apart for so long, we risk our own fragmentation, our potential dissolution.

Daniel, now everything's gone haywire, nothing's in its place. Even the seasons have gotten it wrong. It's ten weeks past Christmas, and spring feels so distant, the summer impossible without having you in it.

I sit for hours out past Pelican Bay thinking of Malibu, how its morning light eclipsed the rest of the day, left the beaches struck with gold and infinite promise—Malibu, where we met, succeeded, then failed, and failed again. Where you constructed a family out of ashes and straw. Where I stood by your side as it crumbled and burned.

How sober we were at the very start, and by the end, how seasoned, having steeped for so long in a dark, bitter brew. But even when defeat was certain, still you smiled and persevered, your eyes firmly fixed on the road.

ON A PHOTOGRAPH OF DORIS BRYNNER, VALENTINO GARAVANI & ELIZABETH TAYLOR

There's Doris Brynner, Yul's second wife,
vamp-eyed, Roman-nosed, my European guide,

and Mr. Valentino, all teeth and brilliantine,
                    the two captured in profile.

Elizabeth, seated between them,
an elegant turn to the camera—

        who knew better the mechanics of posing?—

still beautiful, luminous,
in Valentino lace.

I was probably thinking,
by the time the shutter snapped:

Dove la machina?
                Where's the car?
my only real Italian.

I'd planned our escape from the gala
through a back kitchen door,

the Italian press relentless, vulturous,
entranced by *mysterium tremendum*.

Queen Elizabeth, numinous,
tracking the room with a razor-sharp eye,

fiercely committed to here and now,
scarcely a nod to the past:

        for what good comes
        from enshrining loss?

A plane crash,
a suicide—

a young god
left smashed and bloody
at the end of an endless road.

Track her, adore her, set her free,
but call her by her given name:

Elizabeth, or Bess, even Bessie Mae,
        but never call her *Liz*;

Liz was a name invented by the press,
the name of one of the housemaids.
Only outsiders spoke it.

Something went wrong in our flight arrangements,
booked into Rome on Alitalia,
        a flight with no First Class.

So every time Madam needed the loo,
she'd make her way back through economy,

through clouds of cigarillo smoke,
catcalls, chants of *"La Liz! La Liz!"*

When she returned, she glared at me
through narrowed, violet eyes,
her silence a sufficiently strong corrective.

EILEEN SUCCUMBS TO
COMPLICATIONS
OF THE VIRUS, COVID-19

For nearly fifty years, since boyhood,
I'd thought about how my mother
                            would pass from this world—

a morbid rumination, wondering
                            what force of nature
would have the power, finally, to take her down.

When it happened two years ago, in early April,
she wasn't prepared.

I'd heard fear in her voice
in a phone call two nights before—

unfamiliar fear,
a luxury she'd never allowed herself,
or perhaps, the world never accorded her.

I imagine she was not an easy patient.
She rejected hospice care,
                            although it would have eased her pain,
helped prepare a smooth transition.

Eileen preferred to stick around and fight.
She didn't know any other way.

*

The virus swept through my mother's
                              assisted living complex
just as a late-night fall sent her to hospital,
where she tested positive for Covid.

After she was admitted,
I received regular phone updates from the shift nurses
                                       a thousand miles away.

Then, after two or three "bad nights,"
my mother simply vanished.

Such a hurried departure,
                  certain to bring complications.

*

April 6th, the date of my mother's death.
April 7th, 8th, as if on cue,
                  once evening settled in,

my hands, held in a vice grip,
the fingers splayed, curled into claws,

         bone-crushed, down to the wrist—

too fast, too wild for an arthritis flare,
too quick to abate, after just ninety minutes—

my mother's pain, her essence,
being drawn out of me.

This new absence from the physical plane,
was more than a wind shear, or tropical depression:

Hurricane Eileen,
transition incomplete,
left swirling between worlds.

*

I could feel her unmistakable presence,
as if to distract me from the pain,

wanting me to understand more deeply
this girl from the frozen upstate

who dipped her snowballs in cold water,
let them stand—

then launched the iced projectiles
at innocent strangers
from behind a snowy berm.

Chased, sometimes caught
by furious men, she'd laugh in their faces
as though they were boys.

All in a good day's play.

Later, from behind the veil of marriage,
my mother continued to live this way:
stirring pots, stalking prey—

maintaining absolute control,
causing chaos, then walking away,
                              blameless, unscathed.

*

Days before the virus takes her,
an older, more dangerous version
                              of my mother
comes to me in a dream.

She suggests that I conjure
                  one good memory
of the two of us together,

to remind you, she says, *that I wasn't all bad.*

*

The familiar bugle call,
        the call to the post—

        then, the voice of the announcer
echoing through the grandstand.

Eileen and I look up from our racing forms,
snap our gum, flick our ash.

The horses are entering the track
for the running of the Canandaigua Classic.

Every year, I get to skip school
for the first day of racing at Finger Lakes.

My mother smooths her skirt,
slips her stilettos back on,
walks to the betting window, wheels the 7 horse,
then places my two-dollar bet to show.

She hands me my ticket,
a slip of cheap pink paper, the ink nearly dry.

The memory:
—this day, every year,
        ours alone, my mother's and mine—

redemptive.

                    *

Near the end of the dream,
my mother asks for my forgiveness.

                    Unthinking, I turn away.

I want, just once, to hear her say: *I'm sorry.*

I turn back to respond to her request.

                    But she has vanished.

There is nothing but the aftertaste
of Chesterfield smoke, its bitter ash,
the afternoon sun on my bare neck.

Sharp spikes of sunlight slicing through
            the perfectly manicured, curry-combed
            sienna terre of the oval track.

II

DANGER FACE

—after Jericho Brown

Show me your true self, your danger face.
Drag me into that dark corona.

Drag the light from the distant-most star
To the souls who languish, succubi.

The souls who languish are seeking your light.
The men who love you are men who miss you.

The men who miss you are men who leave you.
The sword and the shield are with you now.

Why do I place myself in danger?
Born to believe in goodness and light.

Those who love goodness and light prevail.
Steel yourself as you look into the maw.

You are nothing, thing-like, before the maw.
Show me your true self, your danger face.

SIMULACRUM

If, on Sunday, we took a drive
out of this sweltering desert heat,

took the Palms-to-Pines Highway to whatever
green and verdant place it spilled us out,

there would not be a single hint of violence

not one untoward move
the whole afternoon and into the evening—

for that is what you expect of me.

*

If I told you the things I am capable of,
there would have to be silence
                    the rest of the day

for cognitive dissonance, tired cliché:
planets off axes, hearts skipping beats—

for that is not who you believe me to be.

*

I come from a long line
of liars, brigands, and thieves, you see.

Most have managed to *marry up*,
        thus, this pantomime of normalcy
    we perform so well.

Under this patina is a gleaming,
                glassed-off patch of ice,
on which we place those
to be tried, exiled, abolished.

The will-to-power defines who we are,
        is more than a propensity,
        is carried in the blood,

is equal to the force
of any family name.

My given name is Josef,
like Mengele, like Stalin.

I call myself Josiah,
after the beneficent King of Judah.

HOMO
—after Lucille Clifton

Why \\ is what I ask myself

maybe it's the \\ homo in me
still trying to get free
            after all \\ these years

mournful decades \\ repeating
to myself in endless \\ dulcet tones

            you are worthy \\ *you are not alone*

so you can die now,
now that you're \\ accepted
no \\ tolerated

as you fly off \\ into some blank
space of whiteness \\ the artist's
            abstract vision of \\ how form
intersects with space

            or some such bullshit \\ until
you are completely erased
from all place and time \\

                    into never having
existed at all

or perhaps \\

use the raw power you culled
from \\ this pandemic
            to plant yourself \\ firmly

with great self \\ assurance
down into \\ the
earth

            immovable flora \\
            redwood blooming \\ the most
                    delicate of blossoms

intractable yet \\ light as willow bark
bending into \\
                    the slightest breeze

        & live \\

& go on living as long
as \\ it pleases you to live

                    not fade away
from \\ heaven's gaze

        never saying \\
                    how

you don't dance

'cause girl

you got music in \\ each tendril
at the tip of \\ every blossom & bloom

and may I say
as I move \\ beyond the hump
of my remaining \\ earthly days

how you rock \\

     how you roll \\

you should stay

IT PAINS ME TO SAY IT

And so, I have not yet thanked you for the generous cache
of books that appeared in my mailbox just after you left
(including a copy of *your* new book, big congrats, by the way!).

To be totally transparent, I should say that I'm not quite sure
exactly *when* you left, what with finalizing my divorce
and all the rigmarole those last few days. Actually,

since we're in a truth-telling mode, I should tell you
that was the week I went to Puerto Vallarta without a word
to anyone, radio silence—took a condo a block from the beach

and hibernated, escaped from the world completely. Well,
truth be told, not *completely*, since that was the week
I met Javier, who's fabulous, whom you'll meet very soon!

So let me say, in all honesty, when I found the books you sent,
I hadn't checked the mail in weeks, no, several months,
to be exact, not since I received that nasty *3-Day Notice to Quit*,

which, quite frankly, freaked me out completely. I mean,
one all-night party, the bed collapses, and suddenly, *Whoa!*
I'm a bad tenant! Lucky for me, your apartment was available.

I hate to ask it, it pains me to say it, but a cable bill arrived,
addressed to *me!* I mean, can you say, *"salt in the wound?"*
Can I count on you to pay it, with your book all published,

and you in the chips?   You *are* a dear.
I don't say it nearly enough.

THE MENDICANT OUTLAW

I gave away my Red Book to poor old Dr. Frank,
all stove up and hot with valley fever. Vain-
glorious, I gave up my ambition to the ages;
then gave up the illusion of having no ambition.
I settled on relinquishing the need to finish first—
first-born son of a first-world nation, privileged
outlaw, charging ahead to change the unchange—
able, do the undone. I gave up my place in
the entering class, went off to be of service
to my father—sold the family business when
he passed away that spring, then spent the next
two years completely tanked. I gave up my will
to some neglectful higher power, then clamored
and tantrummed and took it all back. Found solace
in some forty days devoid of thirst or hunger,
then binged and purged on carnival fare, crashed
your uncle's bacchanal, devoured the roast
and wedding cake, drained every cask of every
decent wine. I sweet-talked my way into a seedy
beachside lair but found no contentment there,
brooked no carnal desires; the fires I'd cherished
were sated and banked. I gave up my place in the
family of things, and lived alone in abject isolation.
Then you came rolling in like a silent tsunami,
inescapable, awash with compassion for those who
truly love the world, who mourn the snowy egret,
sing sonnets to the dawn. You praised the songs
of poets paying homage to the vanished, to the
vanquished, to those who pray in vain to save

the very nearly gone. A bittersweet relinquishment,
this life without the outlaw—he's still appearing
nightly, somewhere far off the mainstage, where
he bucks and brays at the top of his lungs, jockeys
for attention. I hear his exhortations in my dreams.

THE BUDDHA WAITS

From the Buddha, I learned
how to wait, how to fast.

From my mother, I learned
to survive, what to do

when milk is scarce,
how to wrest the teat

from a sleeping child.
Each morning you're away,

I go out to the fields
& worry at the harvest.

The nights you're gone,
I drink too much,

& fight with the kitchen boys
over things of no importance.

Each evening by lamplight,
in crisp white gloves,

I dust the books in your library,
clean the shelves they occupy,

shine the leather bindings
where your name, the same

as your father's name,
is deeply etched in gold.

My father taught me
to live a middling life.

He is old, & tells me
he dreams longingly of death.

In my own dreams, I'm nimble,
quick over the balustrades,

fleet along the rooftops.
My eyes cast a feral light.

But in the harsh glare of afternoon,
we see just who we are:

two aging men with aching backs,
so much like our own fathers.

You bow to the Buddha
who dwells in me,

I bow to the Buddha
of our infirmities.

How hard it has become
to straighten ourselves.

THE FALSE GARDENER

Before you go,
let me tell you this one thing:

> *all last winter and into the spring,*
> *death felt very close to me.*

It's not something I speak of often,
not dinner conversation, cocktail talk—

> there were so many variables at play:

missing you, the you I'd conjured,
the life I'd claimed as mine—

marriage gave me the *how to be,*
a reason to hurl myself into the world

while my heart tried
                    to strike a balance,
to open, cleave to the possible,

> to change at the root,
> attend to the garden,
> left, for the most part, untended.

Through late summer and into the fall,
we rarely spoke. You barely noticed.

I woke early each morning,
went to the garden,
                              moved stealthily
among the stunted plants,

pulling up bindweed, gathering dandelion,
spiriting it away.

I finally left to find relief
        from the terrible wrath of winter,

turned the wattage up past a sensible burn,
acetylene-torched the blue-green ice
beneath my own two feet.

When my guard was well and truly down—

                please understand,   *I was dismembered*—

what had been in hibernation
came roaring back to life—

            a pathogen, a lethal spore
            on a surgeon's scalpel or breathing tube,
            unbidden.

The prospect of death
became real to me then,

            death by suffocation,

my demise no longer
some outlandish, distant notion,

our divorce just one component
of a much more Byzantine plan.

And so began
the time of my *pathology*,

of not being believed,
                    or at best, misunderstood,
whilst you remained devoid
of any deep, caring function.

I was spellbound, paralyzed—
                    that is, until today.

The garden remains, its care and feeding.

I'll gather the hose, the rake and hoe
                    for watering, seeding,

the poison pellets to kill the weeds.

Before you go, let me ask you
                    this one last thing:

you understand, don't you,
that we're not quite finished?

Expect me.

I promise:

        I will not be long coming.

DIVORCE EPISTLES

i.   Exchanges and Elisions

I knew I would find you, I knew I would lose you.
—SPENCER REECE

You walk around in a stranger's skin,
imitating yourself.

Too hard to be with the people you know.
Their words of concern feel hollow.

"I'm sorry," they say,
                 as if someone has died.

"It's OK," you reply,
and begin to explain,

as though helping the *other* to understand
might illuminate the loss,

           or give one of you a quick escape.

"Are you seeing anyone?" they continue.
You start to answer, but stop yourself,
not certain if they mean
               therapist or *paramour.*

What do they think
they're entitled to know, anyway?

You say nothing. If you speak,
you might slip,

            say something hurtful,
only partially intended.

But so what?
It was never your job
to be *acceptable*.

ii.   Theory, Praxis

You call our marriage *a litany of loss.*
I counter, *a catalogue of absences.*

How does one abandon, mourn
such an absence,
                    such a loss?

The old, black screen door echoes,
                    slamming shut behind me.

I turn around just long enough
          to glimpse your face, your eyes—

slightly veiled, narrowed,
watching as I walk away,

          both of us staggered
          by what we have wrought.

iii.   Little Altars

Then, a year in orbit, untethered:

a rented railroad apartment for me,
never fully occupied,

drawers and closets stuffed
with clothes unworn, unattended.

Friends sing odes to the stages of grief,
to the healing power of forgiveness, time;

a *return to normalcy*, they believe,
        is like a deep sigh I've denied myself.

*

But I've been busy acquiring things,
crowding the rooms with artifacts,
            arranging them in groups—

studio pots with lots of flair,
        thick-glazed, jewel-toned;
carvings of wood with unusual burl,

cupboards full of thrift store stoneware,
inconvenient settings for three,

cairns of polished stones,
all of similar heft and hue—

            I'd polish embers if I could—

this is how I live now,
building little altars everywhere
to a vision of us I used to possess,

like a memory of barley the earth once had,

or the promised return to Canaveral
as the doomed capsule hurtles deep into space.

*

I re-arrange the polished stones, the polished eggs,
place the tiny painted egg alone atop the others,

all in perfect symmetry
but lacking deeper meaning,

like this marriage, this couple,
once gorgeous on paper,

now thin and frail as rutted silk.

iv. This Was the Year

you stormed out of the hospital
an hour before they released me—

      the year I made my exit
      from that rehab out west,

no one to guide me
though the whitewashed halls—

the remnants of any good feeling for me
had faded like the memory of your mother

      and I became her suicide:
      near-fiction, not spoken of

something on the roadside
you swerved to avoid—

so sayonara baby
to late confessions

adios to that cold and silent stare—

hail the moral high ground
that became your refuge

long live your book club
your volunteer days

your crippling fear of poverty
impending retirement

or whatever it is
you're planning to do

with the rest of your life
without me in it

v. House Not a Home

The house is settling. Every night,
    the timbers groan, the foundation thuds as it centers on slab.
    Our silences fill with accusations, the continuing contest of
    who's suffered the most . . .

an unlatched gate lets strangers in,
    time replaces bare patches of skin with downy feathers
    that turn to quill, strong enough to support my weight.

I dream of the lift off,
the flight to my hometown,
landing on the Evans Field 40-yard line.

The stands are filled with businessmen, priests,
    mothers of kids I played with once,
garbagemen, councilmen, the tourist town's elite
to whom I'll deliver, in clarion voice

a heady blend of Peter and Paul,
the fisherman,
the learned aesthete:
    my own divorce epistle.

                But battle worn, I conjure only Christopher,
                      my namesake, travelers' icon,
                            now disbarred;

                    and a trace of poor old Jude,
                  patron saint of hopeless cases
          to whom my mother always prayed.

The house has settled,
finally, the judgment signed
the battles won,   or lost,
all weighted, now, the same.

vi. And So I Come Back Into the World

*"Out beyond ideas of wrongdoing and rightdoing there is a field.
I'll meet you there. When the soul lies down in that grass,
the world is too full to talk about."*
—RUMI

It did not come with a trumpet call, or with violins.

It did not come suddenly but dawned gradually, selectively,
displacing blocks of dark matter
               that had held me earthbound.

      It did not come until it was ready,

when the calendar turned on the winter solstice,
then, the start of a new year,
        with old dues paid and scores settled.

It came when I accepted
          the archangels as my guides,

who were prepared to catapult me
                 over any precipice
into a new existence I'd resisted completely:

     free agent, author of my life path.

          And so I come back into the world,

take up the places I have earned or been granted,
the tasks I have delayed or denied,

take down the barriers I have placed between myself
                                        and lifelong friends
in the name of my ineffable sadness,

        and with all the sincerity I can muster,

release myself and others
                from any spiritual or worldly agreements
which no longer serve.

I place the gauntlet back in its keep.

III

THE GOSPEL ACCORDING TO LORENZO THE YOUNGER

I am the unexpected and unforeseen, origin of my name unknown, the mysterium. In the beginning, there were four brothers surrounding a crib, their love and protection already assured.

Fire, Air, Earth, Water, granted me, by their very presence, unencumbered access to the world, to the grace and power of the four elements:

to cleanse, consume, and renew by flame;

to be avian, soaring on waves and currents of air;

to stand firm, steadfast, safely planted in the earth;

to course and flow like a river or stream, and to rest, blissful, oceanic, complete in myself.

Some Latinate influence must have pervaded the very English *Lockes*—the Locke who carved the ornate altar, painted the lost oils, served King Alfred and Anne Boleyn, fought the Revolutionary War on the opposite side of his two sons.

Lorenzo—perhaps the lover of a brother, or my mother's first and secret paramour? More likely, a protégé of my father's, or a fellow inventor—my father, with no formal education, who mastered the telegraph, ran the railroad, and met the need for insulation from the new electric current by creating tiers of ceramic and skirts of thickened glass.

I am the mysterium, the unforeseen and unexpected, origin
of name unknown. In the end, I was alone, floating in a skiff, neither
dead nor alive, in a body of water contained by a shoreline of pine
and poplar, a Scottish loch or an Iroquois lake, cut deep by glaciers or
torn into the landscape by the claw of a giant as he stalked the land,
simian-like,

as my brothers, my father, the sons of my daughters and
I were stalked and finally felled by the weakness of our hearts,
congenital, the inevitability of valve and artery's clogged collapse, an
organ's implosion, the truncated dance—

my father drifting off peacefully in his chair, his pipe still lit
and smoking, and the four elements snuffed out, one by one, until only
I, the youngest, remained.

THE WAITING
—after Galway Kinnell

Wait, he tells me.
Everything will become lovely again.

    —There may be nothing left of me by then, I say.

Even so, he replies.
His eyes crinkle with delight
at his own irony.

    —I am exhausted. Aren't you exhausted? I ask.

I can't quite tell. At 82, what are my choices?

      —You have the joie de vivre of a much younger man.
        You have what I've lost.

He stares down at my left forearm.
Show me that damned tattoo again.

Under my sleeve, these words:

      "I was falling in love with the world,
        and everything in the world was dying."

You see, you've done all this before,
you've loved the world, and you will again.
Things will become possible once more.

—How does one become so wise? I ask.

I gather up my things,
my rucksack heavy with oranges
picked that morning from his orchard.

I bend to him, kiss his brow.
Once outside,

I lean against the wood and iron door
that keeps him safe, alone in his apartments,

    and let the exhaustion blow through me.

I listen for the flute of my own existence,
but hear only the wind
        in the high-above palms.

MILKMAN

At first, I refused.

I saw no sense in being split down the middle,
bifurcated, as if life wasn't already hard enough.

Then, summer's cruel inferno knocked me over,
bent me sideways—not like
the willow's wise concession to the wind,

                        but left breathless,
in the last gasp of obsolescence, like dial tones,
or windmills, or the milkman,

      no longer used or needed,
      and certainly not loved.

Later, past the time of sleep's elision,
when strange, new vistas no longer appeared
before my opiate eyes,

when I finally could distinguish
          dusk from dawn, I understood
how ablations could be bridges,

the string of scars down my chest and belly
like train tracks from the valley
where Guernseys graze

to the lattice of my unlatched door,
where I rise each day
          to whatever labors yet remain.

REJECTION FRACTION

The general consensus
was that I had been recalcitrant,

disinterested, non-compliant.
This was only partially true.

There's a numerical term used
to describe the heart's capacity

to push blood through its channels.
Mine was low, pitifully low, deemed

insufficient, unsuitable for surgery.
So, the cutters rejected me before

I had my say. This was the way
I'd rejected my father, swerved

to avoid the expected collision,
before the words, "You're dead to me,"

could be spoken or heard
and thus, inscribed upon my flesh.

MEDICINE

The sky was ablaze with orange and pink—
they'd shot me full of radioactive,
the better to see my auricles, ventricles.
I didn't need to take my medicine.

The day I came home from the hospital,
I sat under eucalyptus, pine,
wondering how many more summers I'd see—
still, I wouldn't take my medicine.

When kindly you came to attend to me,
brought family, magic—
                    my own menagerie—
I was too gay to take my medicine.

You are a transient luxury—nothing
is permanent, the Upanishads say,
and soon, all of you will leave me.
That's why I don't take my medicine.

Come to my bedside.
Gather around me.
I want to be first to say goodbye.
Brother, bring me my medicine.

VISITOR

Up on the green, fluorescent ward
a young man lies sweating,
                    shivering in a bed
as his body sheds its medicine.

Before the fever breaks,
he looks at me and says:
These bones are only borrowed.

I know the world is a temporary place.
There are times I see
                    the absence of things
more clearly than the thing itself:

the way night deepens
before it leaves
so the morning can fill with light.

The blue mystery
        of my brother's heart—
for some, a portal,
for me, a border closed.

The ferry I missed,
                    last of the day,
leaving me to contemplate
the abbey's grey ruin.

The course and sweep
of my own addiction—
its swift retreat,
        triumphant return.

The familiar ache
of my own borrowed bones,
reminding me
             that I, too,
am only a visitor here.

PICTURE OF HEALTH

The nurse is making me walk, take pills,
do other things I don't want to do.

> They tell me I am healing
> but I feel like I am dying—

what did they find
when they peeled back my breastbone

to lace three veins
onto a disobliging, still-beating heart?—

> too small here, too withered there,
> ancient moonscape, weather-beaten—

my heart no longer a refugee city,
its chambers too blood-starved to be resettled,
vessels too thin to sustain new life.

The picture of health
               is the face we impose
                         on the full Wolf Moon,
half-real, half-imagined—

and so, the relentless march toward death
commences anew in the heart of winter,

the lunar visage, half-visible, half-smiling,
there, in the deep blue distance.

LAZARETTO
—after Lise Goett

I've broken through to longing now,
filled with a grief I have felt before, but never like this.
                                        —RUMI

The grip that comes in the night, rests easy,

then wakes with a stranglehold around the ribs,
taking the breath.

Now add the sharp tang of morning sweat
running in rivulets between shoulder blades—

        a moan arising with every exhale—

then, from behind closed eyes,
the sister-nurse-attendant
                                swathed in cream and white,
her pierced veil, her basin and lance,

the longing for the rush and flow
once the infection is freed from its chamber.

        Longing, its resurrection;
        the heart inflamed, but at rest now.

As the lungs contract,
crystalline fissures thread the tissue,
dark threads against the pink-turned-to-mauve.

A purple cast, vague as moonlight,
comes to crown the lips.

The face of the Beloved appears,
                              as if in a dream.

How the body longs for one more day
as the world closes down around it.

PRAYER FROM CARDIOLOGY

It's not the pain I fear,
nor extinguishment.

I already know how it feels to go out
      like a flame
        deprived of oxygen.

When finally comes my turn to die
I pray you'll grant a holy death—

                        my nightshade, my clavier—

                        you pull opus after opus
                            from my body
                            with your hands.

IV

THE OLDER AMERICAN POET
DIVIDES (HIS) TIME

Here in San Miguel de Allende, where I am growing old, outside the
door behind the gate of Casa Providencia, the cobbled street unfurls
out past the corner tienda where neighborhood children gather after
dark, past the church of San Antonio and into city Centro, to the
turrets and spires of the great, pink cathedral.

Here, in Mexico, because it is ancient, they build houses over
battlegrounds, unmarked graves, long gone dry and cold. Mine is such
a house. I come back to it each November for *Dia de los Muertos,*

    fleeing surgeries, injuries, the dark temptations of
hungry ghosts that haunt my desert door—their satin wings upon my
cheek, webbed with Prussian lace; their faces, Roman catacombs, their
caverns, deep and distant:

       I must not go there alone.

I've all but forsaken the glitter and rust of that sweltering desert town,
the golden dust that shrouds the air like sacrament or curse. I take to
my bed, won't call or keep a calendar, can't bear the risk of stopping
time by chronicling the hours:

 for what if time won't start again, if the nature of the universe,
 our ultimate destiny, is *entropy?*

Here, at Providencia, the timbre of the tin-roof rain disarms and lulls
us, positive ions charging the air; I lean in to hear my husband whisper
as sleep overtakes him, a nightly cache of truths revealed—

       he's saying—

he must be saying: *don't be afraid, I'll pull you from your demon dreams,
make time begin again.*

THE DEAD (*Calaveras Literarias*)

The dead do not inhabit Woodlawn Cemetery,
nor the burial mounds on Boughton Hill,

no matter how finely cut the stone,
no matter if found undisturbed.

The dead are not occupied
with filing back taxes, making gratitude lists,

applying for temporary or permanent visas—
some of the more recently dead

may tweak the tungsten for attention,
or stir the linen canopy that shrouds the marriage bed.

And it must be said
that some are trapped between two worlds—

                    swimming in a sea of stone

on Day of the Dead, the gates of heaven
fling themselves open to ancestors,

parents, the violently taken,
spirits of children gone too soon—

last night, the ghost of *mi Madre* appeared,
un-altered, festooned with marigold blossoms,

standing in our kitchen, raiding the fridge
for a cold Corona—

the chihuahua guard dog, Stella,
watched her from the doorway,

        and all of us were dead

making not a single sound.

RETURNING TO AVERNO

—after Louise Glück

You die when your spirit dies.
You might stand up from a café table,
shift your weight onto a weakened hip,
and crumble like a scone, tumbling down
a flight of stairs. I remember the days
before my body betrayed me,
stepping smartly along Lexington
on my way to some meeting or event,
blithely bypassing others on the street,
so keen on my own self-importance.
I had plans, big plans, big ideas—
nothing seemed too far-fetched or
out of reach, so great was my certitude,
my sense of purpose. It was, to be sure,
the arrogance of youth, but essential
to the tasks which lay before me.
The decimation. I don't know how
to tell you this. I don't know whether
you need to know, or if you can even
empathize. I wanted to run out
into the street, scream *no, no, no,*
and I did, in my dreams. Now, I may
not know anymore the word for chair,
but I can sit happily in one for hours,
gazing out a random window, wool-
gathering, or watching people as they

come off the plane, vaguely dissociated,
time-obsessed, desperate for the next
text or call confirming their pick-up spot.
I was like that once, on the move,
a hunter, one of the pack. These days,
the young ones in white coats and sweats
nod, share glances they think I don't see,
ask me if I still practice. I tell them yes,
I still practice—that I am, in fact, at
the height of my powers.

JAPAN

I dream I am having a dream from which I slowly awaken. In the dream, I am in Japan. The air is crisp and clean, newly born. Pain, my constant companion, is absent, leaving me feeling strangely alone, without a body. I am a wisp of aromatic smoke, nothing more. Blue smoke rising in the thin mountain air.

My father is dying. I can hear him calling out to me from a far distance. His voice is tentative, plaintive, apologetic for his failings. His many failings. And I think, *I must be in Japan because my father sounds so far away.*

I love my father, but he does not love me. For this, I resent him deeply. To him, I was an unnecessary child; my very existence diverted focus from him, from his needs, which were primal and necessary.

But now, on his deathbed, I accord him the respect I have always withheld. I walk a fine line between *duty* and *truth*. The tension is electrifying. I think to myself:

This is what death must be like:

inevitable, irresistible, yet utterly terrifying.

Creation, in all its perfection, suddenly set ablaze.

My father is dying. Yet there is no heaven for him to occupy. Only worlds within worlds, expanding out beyond time into deep space. I try to imagine what it's like to have had a body, then to relinquish it at death. To go from being a wisp of smoke to the enclosure of a body, once again, at rebirth.

How disconcerting it must be, like visiting Japan for the first time. Everything turning in on itself, everything upside down.

I am at the end of a long, disconnected dream where neither *death* nor *longing* are ever acknowledged. This has been my life, until now. I have always longed for my father's love. My longing extends out beyond the universe, outside the realm of time, transcends its initial object.

It is a plume of blue smoke rising high above Shimogamo Temple—*I am rising, a wisp of blue*—up and up, through the clean mountain air. To a place where dreams are blown into existence.

I LIVED FOR ART, I LIVED FOR LOVE

I dreamed I walked barefoot all the way to your house in the snow.
Everything was the blue of smudged ink and you were still alive.
There was even a light the shade of sunrise inside your window.
                                        —OCEAN VUONG

As I approached the house, I could hear the soft click of your record player and the dark hum of a woman's voice, shaded in blue, emanating from your window. If I had to describe in detail the color, the hue of the voice, of the moon-shadow and the moon, I would say *indigo*.

I could hear the movement of the music as waves of sound refracted off the snowbanks around me, chords progressing from minor to major then back again, minor seven chords scaling upward to create tension that the voice would then resolve, bringing all back into order with the solidity of a major fourth, letting the ear rest for a moment, just long enough for the listener to identify the song—no, the aria—it was "Vissi D'Arte" from Puccini's opera, "Tosca."

There was no doubt as to the singer's identity, even without a closer, more nuanced listening, I knew who it was, who it had to be. You would be waiting for that penultimate phrase, the one you'd heard hundreds of times before, where the singer eschews the need for a breath—and all other singers require one—in the middle of the word "signore." Then, the voice takes two steps down, perfectly balanced, to end the phrase in the most exquisitely controlled pianissimo.

It could only be Caballé.

In the dream, as in our waking life, you were a creature of extreme habit, easy to predict. Years earlier, I knew to expect your terse note when, post break-up, I tried to abscond with my favorite recording:

The album of Puccini arias is not a gift to you. Please see that it is returned, posthaste. As Tosca discovered, "living for art, living for love" does not necessarily guarantee the best, most hoped-for result.

*

In the dream once again, walking barefoot in the snow, walking backwards, entranced by the blueness of the air yet longing for the sun-risen promise of being there with you, warm, golden, in your room, in your arms. You were still alive. Caballé had yet to sing that last phrase. The air and sky had turned from cobalt to navy to a new shade of blue, just shy of a dark turquoise.

I could still breathe freely, could still hear that aria not as an indictment of God and of my own life, but as a work of art separate and apart from me, from the life I'd lived and would go on living. None of us would remain as we were, flung out of one dimension into another, but that is another dream entirely.

DIVA

She is alone on a stage, held in an arc of blue-tinged light from a single caged bulb atop a lamppost—the light is harsh and unforgiving. In the pixelated photographs I keep on my phone, we are similarly held, as if in amber, in a flash, in a spark of unnatural, manmade light, unmoving, unmoved, facsimiles of ourselves, the selves we once were or purported to be, nothing of earth or sky in our mien, no cirrus, no humus, no night-bloom of jasmine redolent in our hair.

We are reduced to pixels arranged on an incandescent screen, bereft of bone and sweat, no chemical cascade that leaves behind a lover's particular flavor, her unmistakable musk. Alone, orphaned, like the woman onstage preparing to sing, her intake of breath expanding her diaphragm, lifting her torso while pushing the small heft of her body down, grounded, held in the spotlight.

In moments like these, I envision a woman, one I know to be composed of flesh and blood; no solid object—nothing broken or petrified, shocked into entropy—could ever pass through her, could ever produce that frequency—*listen, she is about to sing*—from the bone-against-bone of her beginning to the steady gain of strength from song to song—

the sweat on her temple, the clutch of her two hands on the microphone, and she becomes, once again, widowed, solitary, each note containing all the pathos of a full life, richly lived, an existence that was nothing she could have planned.

And now, as she steps into the golden limelight that envelops the stage, she is amorphous, formless, as light and lithe as a girl half her age—then, the doyenne lamenting her own lost youth, the transience of beauty—she is trying to tell us, *believe*.

THE GOSPEL ACCORDING TO DON LORENZO THE FIRST

From the fisherman sprang the fisherwoman from whom emerged an embodied light, and the light was harnessed and shorn of its beams and consigned to steerage where it languished

until its spark of brilliance began to consume itself in order to remain present in the world. Every prayer for good and proper measures to assure its continuance fell on Gaia's deaf ear.

So the light dissected itself into fragments and waves, the power to do so gleaned from the ardent prayers of others and intervention of the archangels,

the better to survive in pieces and parts, to be later reconjoined when Gaia, the source of all, awoke, and Kosmos, too, gathered itself into wakefulness,

and thus arose

hope,

verdant in the face of fire, such that the embodied light was lifted above the waterline where it had floated, prismatic, resting, awaiting its time.

PROVIDENCIA

A steel-gray plate of sky
presses down
on this December morning.

There's the promise
of approaching showers,
perhaps as soon as afternoon—

the patio chairs in tarpaulin coats,
the new umbrella pinioned and bound,
no need for protection from noonday sun.

And on this day, I'm miles away,
consorting with a sorceress.

She is comfortably ensconced
in her country house, a priestess
who shuffles cards, speaks in tongues,
                    evaluates the light:

Let it hit you and open you,
                    up on the roof,
the light all soft and luscious,

go up there and sit under the sky . . .
let your father 'take the thorns away,'
as he tells me he's willing and able to do . . .

forgive the Church, forgive yourself,
for it's finally clear that you want to live.

Later that evening, just past midnight,
awakened by footsteps pounding on metal,

I look down from the third-floor roof
on this subdivided plot of land,
             once known as "Providencia,"

and now incised, divided
among *la familia* Lopez.

Some years ago, Juan Carlos
bought one Lopez sibling's
             quarter share of the land,

and built this house for his sister and mother,
both lost to age and illness
before they could take up residence.

He finished the house with love and care,
the well-mitered beams and fine-fitted ironwork

reaching from the ground-floor atrium
to the open sky, colonial style.

I look down upon
the remaining Lopez dwellings:

two shanties, an open plaza between them,
lit by a single hanging bulb,

a ladder up to the ironwork
that separates our properties
and anchors our home-grown vines.

I watch the Lopez neighbor girl,
all of seven or eight, as she climbs the ladder—

      did a young girl's footsteps rouse me from sleep,
      or a dream visitation from my father?

The girl takes hold of a sheet of tin
jutting from her roof—

with a slam and flick, a grip and shake,
she makes thunder for the neighborhood.

How much, I wonder, to extend the iron
up beyond the ladder's reach,

closing off the open space
that links their place and mine?

      Amid the din, I calculate the cost.

But simple sheets of filigreed iron
raised up and placed between us

won't erase the bonds, ancient and new,
between familia Lopez
      and familia Emerson-Gordon.

We've taken the view,
   the best of the air,

but providence herself decrees
we share the numinous light.

TWELVE O'CLOCK SHADOW

Write this: I will die in Mexico,
waiting in line for a *café de olla*
just before noon on a weekday morning,

face down on a crowded sidewalk,
clipping my head on an ancient curb.

An ordinary day,
unlike any day we've seen before—
          a cup of sky turned upside down,
settling around us, a pall of bluest blue;

a cross between turquoise
                              and cobalt, this blue—
Talavera Blue, the hue you see all over town,
a not-accidental, consequential shade of blue.

                    *

Write this: it was yesterday I landed at Léon,
and I wonder, in this netherworld:

did I travel any distance,
                    or merely fly in circles,
my trip a non-necessity, dissolving in the rain?

It was my father,
or the ghost of my father,
waiting at the jetway, his face grey and oval,

          a dove's egg, bland and smooth,

with a mouth that moved but did not speak,
until he spat, at my feet, a spate of blue feathers—

blue the blue of robins' eggs—
            only then did I awaken.

                    *

Write this: *Why must I be the one to die?*
It's a Monday morning, hours past dawn.
My cup is full: a caffeinated brew
            of cinnamon, sweet bark, cherry seed,
adorned with sprigs of lavender.

C.W. Emerson did not die today.
There he goes, Old Doc himself,
limping down Calle Libertad—we expected
            a commotion, an ambulance or two—

but there's only this crystalline sky,
and this sun—*mijo*, what a day!—
mothers walking children home
                    from nursery school at noon,

the sky so blue you can taste it, almost;
a day so sublime it's cliché, and a shame
            not to be at the Jardin, in the square,
on the road to Damascus, or Mandalay,

or Dolores Hidalgo,
where church bells are ringing
                    to celebrate Monday,
an everyday, inconsequential
twelve o'clock noon.

        And I am alive to hear it.

ACKNOWLEDGMENTS & NOTES

The following poems appeared or are forthcoming in these print and on-line journals, sometimes in slightly different versions or with different titles:

2 Bridges Review: "The Buddha Waits"
december: "homo"
Harvard Review: "The Gospel According to Don Lorenzo the First," and "The Gospel According to Lorenzo the Younger"
The American Journal of Poetry: "Divorce Epistles"
The New Guard: "The Waiting"
Passenger: "It Pains Me to Say It"
Schuylkill Valley Journal: "Visitor"

"American Seasons" was selected as a finalist for the 2020 International Proverse Poetry Prize, and appeared in the anthology, *Mingled Voices 4: International Proverse Poetry Prize* (Proverse Hong Kong, 2020), edited by Gillian & Verner Binkley.

"Danger Face" is in the form of a "duplex," a form originated by Jericho Brown, and lines six and seven are quotes from Brown's poem, "Duplex (I Begin With Love)."

"Des Rêves Fantastiques (Les Fantômes)" owes a debt to the poem, "How We Got Into This" by Cecilia Woloch.

"Divorce Epistles": The epigraph that precedes "Exchanges and Elisions" is from "ICU" by Spencer Reece. The epigraph that precedes "And So I Come Back Into the World" is from Rumi, translated and adapted by Coleman Barks (*The Essential Rumi*, 1997).

"Eileen Succumbs to Complications of the Virus COVID-19" was a finalist for the 2022 Montreal International Poetry Prize, and appears in *The Montreal Poetry Prize Anthology 2022*, edited by Eli McLaren (Véhicule Press, 2023).

"homo" was inspired by Lucille Clifton's poem, "hag riding," and the opening lines are quoted from the first lines of the poem.

"How I Came to Be Myself" appeared in my chapbook, *Off Coldwater Canyon* (The Poetry Box, 2021). It is inspired by Justin Boening, and the poem's final line is a quote from Boening's poem, "How I Came to Rule the World."

"I Lived for Art, I Lived for Love": The epigraph is from Ocean Vuong's "Notebook Fragments," *Night Sky with Exit Wounds*.

"Lazaretto": The epigraph is from Rumi, translated and adapted by Coleman Barks (*The Essential Rumi*, 1997).

"Lazaretto," "Milkman," "Picture of Health," "Prayer from Cardiology," "Providencia," "Rejection Fraction," "Returning to Averno," "The Gospel According to Don Lorenzo the First," "The Gospel According to Lorenzo the Younger" and "The Gospel According to Mercie Peer" comprise *The Thoracic Diaries*, co-winner of *Poetry International's* Summer Chapbook Contest 2023, which will appear as a portfolio in *Poetry International*, Issue 30, 2024-25.

"Returning to Averno" was inspired by Louise Glück poem, "Averno," and the opening line is quoted from the first line of the poem.

"The Gospel According to Mercie Peer" is inspired by my great-grandmother Mercie Peer Locke (1866-1952), wife of my great-grandfather Fred M. Locke (1861-1930), who was known as "The Father of the Porcelain Insulator."

"Twelve O'Clock Shadow" owes a debt to César Vallejo and Donald Justice.

I am greatly indebted to Connor Wolfe and their team at Wayfarer Books, to Homebound Publications, Tupelo Press, the poets and faculty at the Tupelo Truchas Poetry Conference and San Miguel de Allende Poetry Week, and all of the generous, talented poets who run poetry marathons with me.

Thanks and love to Marc Hulett, Adrienne Starr, Michael Sterling, Francene Eguren, Wesley Detwiler, Christine Curry, Jason Wilkinson at San Miguel Web Design, Romina Perez Garibay, Stella Evans, Jason Pettinato, Gloria Belendez Ramirez, Blas Falconer, Robert Carr, Lana Hechtman Ayers, and the guiding light that is Cecilia Woloch.

My deep gratitude to Lise Goett, poetry doula extraordinaire, who brought kindness, grace and wisdom to this project.

Finally, thanks to Scott Gordon for his abiding love, which keeps me safe in the face of every danger, real or imagined.

ABOUT THE AUTHOR

C.W. Emerson's work has garnered numerous international accolades, including two awards from Poetry International: the C.P. Cavafy Poetry Prize (2018) and co-winner of the 2023-24 Summer Chapbook competition. Emerson's poetry and literary criticism have been featured in esteemed publications such as *Harvard Review, Oxford University Press, Greensboro Review, Tupelo Quarterly*, and more. He is the author of a chapbook, *Off Coldwater Canyon* (The Poetry Box, 2021), and the prize-winning portfolio, *The Thoracic Diaries*, forthcoming from Poetry International.

Emerson's poetry was a finalist for The Montreal International Poetry Prize (2020), and shortlisted for the International Beverly Prize for Literature (2019). His work has been anthologized in several poetry compilations containing themes relevant to the LGBTQIA+ communities.

Dr. Emerson is a retired clinical psychologist, and divides his time between southern California and San Miguel de Allende, Mexico.

Visit his website at
theolderamericanpoet.com

At Wayfarer Books we believe poetry is the language of the earth. We believe words—shaped like rivers through wild places—can change the shape of the world. We publish poets and writers and renegades who stand outside of mainstream culture—poets, essayists, and storytellers whose work might withstand the scrutiny of crows and coyotes, those who are cryptic and floral, the crepuscular, and the queer-at-heart. We are more than just a publisher but a community of writers. Our mission is to produce books that can serve as a compass and map to all wayfarers through wild terrain.

w a y f a r e r b o o k s . o r g